Plea for Convivence

Ghislaine Alajouanine
Correspondent Member of Institut de France

PLEA FOR CONVIVENCE
SHORTCOMINGS AND FAILURES OF HYPERCONNECTED SOCIETIES

Preface by Pierre Brunel
Professor Emeritus (Paris IV-Sorbonne),
Member of the Institute

Postscript by Dominique-D Junod (Arbell)
Dr. in Political Science, Lic. University of Geneva

*

Translated from French by Jigisha Leclair

hermann
Depuis 1876

"The old world is dying away and the new world struggles to come forth, making room for monsters in this semi-darkness".

Antonio Gramsci

PREFACE

by Pierre Brunel
Professor Emeritus (Paris IV-Sorbonne),
Member of the Institute

What is convivence? the art of "living together, in harmony". This is the definition, based on the etymology (cum-vivere), which is given by Ghislaine Alajouanine to this word, right from the beginning of her book (p. 12). But in 2004 already, Florence Delay, whom she quotes right from the initial lines (p. 7), mentioned the time when the French Academy, on her initiative, introduced convivence inside the illustrious Dictionary, but concluded by "this moment devoted to harmony over emotion, which seems to be overwhelming, when the hope of living together is lost". 1986 onwards, Robert Maggiori published a book entitled De la Convivance with Editions Fayard, quoted by Ghislaine Alajouanine. She herself acknowledged that "our postmodern societies which are supposedly hyper-connected, have never distended the social tie up to such a point" and wanted to underline the word conviviality to revive the hope of living together, following a hard observation and analysis of the evils that strike us". (I am quoting the back cover).

The word "convivence" doesn't date back to the 21st century and the apparent neologism is actually a reinvented word. Reinvented from the Spanish word Convivencia, quoted by Ghislaine Alajouanine, page 45 where she refers to Andalusia between the seventh and twelfth century.

In *Littré*, the absence of conviviality, I find convivant: a term from ecclesiastical history. It is addressed to those who live together, in certain convents of Italy. And Gaffiot's dictionary refers to convivere in the Seneca text, as it is not only a matter of eating together but living together.

So, the word has a history, the thing as well. Just like Ghislaine Alajouanine (p. 8) writes, "more or less distant in the history of mankind, conviviality personifies a reality, a way of life that promotes complex and multi-cultural societies to coexist". She sketches out a historical picture and the example that struck me most is that of Emir Al-Andalus, due to whom, "after the conquest of Andalusia by the Arabs during the seventh century, each one in Al-Andalus was able to freely practice his or her own religion and preserve his or her place of worship" (p. 46).

Indeed, an example to mull over in today's world more than ever, as it is mired by divisions and outbreaks of violence. It is essential to learn to live together, in a world which is considered to be "a global village", and the idea of conviviality must be readapted to the modern era (p. 55). In this "planetary framework" (p. 57), "conviviality will aim to rekindle this flame of living together, this faith that we share, namely a common destiny". This doesn't exclude diversity, and Ghislaine Alajouanine recalls that Fernand Braudel, wished for this when he wrote *The Identity of France* (2000) and wrote: "Let France be called diversity!"

Philological reflection and historical reflection lead to philosophical reflection. Ghislaine Alajouanine firmly channels this by seeking the exact definition of certain words, such as secularism (p. 60–67), equality (p. 70–73), fraternity (p. 73), dialogue (p. 74–75).

It all begins with the family, which is "the first circle of conviviality in which a human being shall evolve in the course of his life" (84-85). I couldn't help but appreciate the position which is given to the role of grandparents (p. 89), at the university. In 2016, Ghislaine Alajouanine decided to create a "Chair of Convivence" under the high patronage of Unesco, which now exists, bound to the University of Saarland, a chair of conviviality, Europa Grande Région under the leadership of Valérie Deshoulières and I had the opportunity to head the doctoral dissertation thesis at the University of Paris-Sorbonne.

But of course, I couldn't help but think about Academies, at Plato's Akademia in the Academos Garden, about the five Academies of Institut de France, which includes ours, in this place which favors exchanges and conviviality, where we end up being a promising example of a space promoting conviviality, a listening space for everything which is dealt in this book by Ghislaine Alajouanine, like morality and politics.

***

In 2004, the French Academy created a new word. The person behind this initiative was a woman, namely Florence Delay, an academician who stated: "Thursday during last spring, the company that I am pleased to represent this fall came up with a new word in their dictionary: the word *convivence* [...]. Please forgive me while I highlight this moment devoted to harmony over the seizing emotion of losing any hope of living together".

Convivence: this word mainly expresses hope. The one of the French Academy, mine... but ours too. The one of reshaping our social ties and our desire of living together, building a harmonious society together. Words are full of invisible strength. They are a weapon, they are so powerful that one doesn't even suspect their ability to build or destroy. As persuasively demonstrated by the philosopher, Jean-Pierre Faye in his masterwork called "Les Langages totalitaires", words sweep along concepts and weave comprehensions that people use later to conceive and implement their policies.

Jean-Pierre Faye has examined the vocabulary of the *Total State* and of the *final solution* to get the destructing power of some words up to speed, which at a first glance seemed trivial, harmless but around which a mythology was gradually founded, the one of totalitarian Nazi or Fascist ideologies… Let's hope that the positive power of another word, namely convivence, could help develop a whole new and humanist ideology. This book has the sole aim of spreading it around.

***

What do we know about convivence? This term may be new in the French language; however, its concept and application go back for centuries. An era which is rather distant in the History of mankind. Convivence personified a reality, an art of living which helped complex and multi-cultural societies to live together. To take things up a notch: the periods where convivence prevailed were synonymous with appeasement and progress. There are reasons for recapturing this ancient neologism. Re-inventing, re-discovering the term convivence, its addition to the French Academy's dictionary at the beginning of our millennium is not just a coincidence. We are modestly trying to respond to a demonstration of necessity but also to a crisis.

I am not here to weigh down my fellowmen with rebukes nor to lecture them, even if what I am going to say might not be appreciated. I am here to make a statement and share my experiences and encounters which have helped me learn about *living together.*

Nowadays, a flourishing terminology counters convivence: unfortunately, other words seem to proliferate in our speech today. Words personifying exclusion, fatal words, words which highlight the rejection of the Other. You are certainly aware of these, as one keeps saying them repeatedly (unless we invent them): these terms have to do with islamophobia, negrophobia, anti-Semitism, homophobia, xenophobia. We have all heard about them and of anti-white racism, anti-black racism, anti-Arab, anticlericalism and misogyny. These words are all evidences of the troubled times in which we live: an era of division. Curiously, this rupture seems to arise during an era which is supposedly hyper-connected.

Either way, we try to create theoretical and vague barriers through these words, to portray the Other person's fear, regardless of the person's gender, faith, social class and clothes. But all the while defining this *Other* through categorical terms which instil fear, one doesn't even bother getting to know the latter and understanding this person's motivation. All these biting words, that are supposed to define communities between which we believe to distinguish, add a great deal of ambiguity and encourage additional conflation which keeps enhancing confusion and division. Failure to put up with one another, takes over us. These superficial and insulting words are harmful as they encapsulate and create division unknowingly, all the while ignoring the categories which they claim to mark out. Provided that these barriers actually exist.

Many of us for example, are convinced that all Arabs are Muslims and that Muslims are all Arabs. However, the largest Muslim country is in Asia: not in North Africa or the Middle-East, not even in the Arabian Peninsula. One can find the highest proportion of those who pray to Allah in Indonesia.

The fact that I am insisting on this specific gross simplification, that I am quoting it first, doesn't mean that I wish to focus my talk on the Muslim community. Do not perceive this as any kind of favouritism, and even less as an attempt to exclude or single out the sons of Islam. It would be a very paradoxical thing to do! My intention is to reunite-not point out and even less victimize a community. There are other shortcuts of such kind, which are as fatal and full of ignorance.

Convivence needs a new lease of life to fight against this ignorance; as the latter is a response to the lack of love, a shared emergency. It's a warning signal that has already been triggered by some pioneers. It's re-emergence in our vocabulary highlights the lack of such expressions as: "living in harmony with each other", "art of living together", "capacity to live harmoniously", "coexist harmoniously" …Regardless of the way we decide to define convivence, the latter only wishes to be given a tangible form through actions and concrete solutions. Furthermore, its diverse definitions prove that its concept is a modern acceptation which is still emerging, unfinished, still in progress and I hope full of potential. Nevertheless, you'll notice that all these definitions are in keeping with one another, as they all respect the Latin root, from which convivence originated: cum vivere, live together in harmony.

How did we end up here? What are the signals which force me to establish this sad fact? Before talking to you about periods of history during which convivence flourished, before suggesting the solutions for this collapse that threatens us, it is important first and foremost

to describe and recognize the evil, its sources,
its symptoms, otherwise we won't be able to
prevent the latter.

G. Alajouanine

THE EVIL THAT WE INFLICT UPON OURSELVES

*When the mercantile mind gets
the upper hand on the Spirit and writings
are taken at face value.*

There are some unwise forces due to which we have forgotten what the art of living with the Other was all about. Through our churches, our means of communication, our way of consuming, we've been fooled, while being lead to believe that it was for our good. We were imperceptibly confined in a "jailed soul", which is more frightful than the feudalism of ancient times.

Children of the "city" we have regressed together. Instrumentalization of our dreams and values by spirits who are greedy for power and money, has reduced our beliefs to a superficial appearance, an enticement which doesn't reflect the historic and political realities of community life in any way whatsoever. This harmful instrumentalization, this deterioration of spirit proclaims to be life-saving, promises solutions as simple as the underlying anger which claims to free us, but which actually controls us. This counters the original message which is advocated by our Holy scriptures, all our laws and authority. Under the guise of promoting them, it has nothing to do with our ideals.

Nationalisms

Since the blood bath of the "Great War", which devastated Europe and wore out all the nations across the world, the scale of massacres has considerably surpassed all the conflicts of the past. Before 1914, and even more since, nationalism has only intensified the regional peculiarities that were raised to the rank of races, justified by genetics as an excuse for the mass slaughter. We had to proudly put ourselves in the firing line and defend the motherland. We were pitted against one another in the name of symbols, which were sung lyrically but the latter hid a more down to earth reality rather than promising patriotic impetus. Let us recall that France found its justification for the Great War in the hatred for the Fritz; but it was mainly about demolishing a competitor who was coming in the way of other industrial powers. Let us also recall that bringing the German Empire to its knees sowed the seeds of the worst of all wars, the one which followed the Great War, a quarter of a century later. Therefore, this relentlessness in revenge was not a solution.

To spark off our hatred, we turned the neighbour into a different being, a barbaric thing. They were caricatured as a wild monster, an unfamiliar species. Take a look at the newspapers from the beginning of the 20th century, the propaganda posters of that era. The enemies were portrayed as spiders, rats, frogs, vultures. One would quickly forget that those in the opposite trench were as human as us. Only humans are capable of such things. We were also made to forget that each faction often believed in the same God. Every opposing person believed to be enlightened, chosen, the only one borne with Reason; each nation was so blind that they destroyed one another. Each one found an explanation of their own exaltation through the other's cruelty.

After all this, why should I be putting these sentences in the past?

We've been divided since centuries. This sick ballet has made way into this new century. As the past years have gone by, one has noticed that nations have withdrawn into themselves.

This movement has only built up; the new leaders question the union which was believed to be something solid, the latter backtracked on exchange agreements and claimed to find salvation through withdrawal. The people elected or nearly elected those whose thinking is a lot like the brown plague which spread through Europe during the 30's.

Hostile communitarism now seems to appear throughout continents and this isn't the first time in History. Is it really a coincidence when the survivors of Shoah try to warn us today, making us understand that a sudden outbreak leads us to the extremes which they perceive as signs of their negative memories? Today's atmosphere is as harmful as it was before the Reich advent. Will it be at its peak tomorrow?

Let's not forget the mistakes which were committed by our ancestors, their attempts to reject our neighbors, breaking ties with them, evicting those who seemed responsible for the sufferings created by others, appointing scapegoats or even annihilating them. None of these brilliant actions improved the condition of the people who implemented them. Due to their talent pool leaving, this often led to serious decline, loss of nations who carried this on but also to the worst holocausts. If all this war and hatred had been so efficient and if they had actually brought happiness and peace to nations, we would know about it.

We could describe this as old-fashioned talk. We could say that these arguments are nothing but residues of ancient times, disconnected fears of reality for the current world. One could argue that our veterans cry wolf as they live in their memories, in their withered youth; they keep repeating the misdeeds of the past, but they don't know what they are talking about anymore as they don't have a grip on the modern language.

One could retort that these propagandas certainly wiped out the world decades ago, at the dawn of mass communication, but that we are now much more clear-sighted when we come across simplistic images, given that we have become accustomed to the media which has immunized us against advertising manipulations, that we just don't believe everything like our naive ancestors.

Do we really think that we are capable of sorting things out, by dint of being exposed to the unbridled flow of the information highway, this constant dataflow which deluges our screens?

Blaming ancestors for their ignorance is lacking perspective. We will get the chance to talk about the duty of remembrance which could save us, the importance of listening to those people who experienced life themselves before we were even born.

Divide and rule

Methods of modern marketing-the one where we are brainwashed through its omni-presence, the one which strives to nourish our fears, our insecurities through direct and repetitive messages-these have given rise to Pavlovian reflexes and compulsive actions within us. Let's not forget that this modern way of selling things to us, which we think we need, originated from notions that are as unclear as the propaganda system defined by Goebbels. This brainwashing works on our dirty ego, rubbing the latter up the right way and just like a Machiavellian consumerist, reducing us into distinct units, to better control our consumption habits. *So, buy, buy, because you're worth it, the waves keep repeating this to us. They say, you're worth it more than the other person. The desire to own dominates you. You go to work so that you can afford this fool's paradise, which makes you drool.*

This system has turned into a caricature of a basic premise of the market economy, advocated by Adam Smith: it's more advantageous to sell a product in small quantities to several people rather than sell in bulk; one yields a bigger profit as the merchandise is split into individual portions. This *modus operandi* has gotten refined with time; it has taken up a more pervasive dimension, with the emergence of the electronic media.

Measuring instruments watch over our doings and actions, our habits are assessed, one watches over everything we do. No, this is not a paranoid delirium nor a conspiracy theory. It's a fact. A selling technique. Big Data analysis of our interactions on social networks and the Internet sites on which we browse helps commercial companies target the products that we shall see emerging in advertising spaces, but also on our screens.

We have stepped into an Orwellian era that is much more pernicious than a declared dictatorship, as espionage now takes place without any kind of repression. Our actions are analyzed through the help of a database to anticipate our future needs. We are observed like guinea pigs to better decide what to sell to us, what to expose us to and show the products which have a greater chance of honing our desires on our crystal displays. One has even invented planned obsolescence, to be sure that we won't have a choice but to buy these drugs one sells us, as they won't last as much as they did before.

Even worse, we have ourselves turned into products. We are assessed in the light of our profitability or the costs we generate. We are nothing but indications, figures, flesh machines. These equations don't take our emotional charges into account anymore, not to mention our dignity. Where is there room to dream in this statistical world?

This way of non-thinking has made way in all the areas of our lives and has even split us away with our families. This deconstruction has got the upper hand on the fundamental social structures of living together, where the taste for community blossomed a long time ago. Our screens, our individualized means of communication make us turn a blind eye on our surroundings.

It's not surprising that we aren't able to recognize another person's sensitivity, as our very own is inadequate. Do we still know how to contemplate? Do we still know how to discover? To take time to identify the same features as ours in others and rediscover that the Other is nothing but another us? Are we going to forget all about our fellowmen as quickly as when we switch channels, when they don't interest us anymore? This already seems to be the case when we examine the habit of consumer sites or dating application: all it takes is a finger nudge, to slide through photos of poor people who have a hard time finding love, they are reduced to nothing but mere commodities of mass consumption.

Argument or Propaganda?

By making us break the habit of pooling in our resources, we have forgotten the meaning-and the benefits-of sharing. By individualizing us, by making us believe that we are enriched through our own possessions, we have internally impoverished ourselves.

Dissecting our humanity doesn't just restrict the way in which we consume manufactured products and services. But it is also about the ideas that one makes us consume; information is shoved down our throats at a rapid-fire speed. Consumerism has surpassed our current consumption habits; it has spread to our souls.

Our screens have provided us with the gift of impatience, immediacy, the compulsive desire to achieve things in a nanosecond, regardless of the quality of what we obtain, as long as it is in a flash. By satisfying our needs through the power of a simple click, we have lost the patience of putting things in perspective or worrying about critical thinking. We live in the era of "ready-to-think", which is the complete opposite of Thinking.

We don't even take the time to sort things out anymore, to separate the good from the bad, to form an opinion in a completely self-sufficient manner. We absorb and consume speedy information, we guzzle down facts to such an extent that we forget what we just swallowed a second ago. The main aim is to find thrills. An illusion of ecstasy. An ersatz of evasion.

This way of believing every single word without even trying to understand, is chipping away at the foundation of democracy, as we believe everything we hear without even trying to detect the true intentions or reasons due to which the messages are sent. The temporary overabundance of information, brain bombing through non-events, accusations, unverified rumours or statements that are hastily tossed, affect our critical thinking.

Thus the recent American presidential election was extremely foul. The democratic debate was distorted during the campaign, it was put on the back burner by third-class accusations which were virally passed along on social networks. This in fact encouraged President Obama to state: "If we aren't serious when it comes to facts, about things which are true and which aren't, especially during the age of social networks when so many people receive information in a jiffy on their telephone, if we cannot differentiate between serious arguments and propaganda, in that case we have a problem". Lawrence Lessig, Law professor at Harvard, rubbed it in: "The social networks need to admit the difference between selling technological gizmos and broadcasting information on elections".

Therefore, we have made our way into the era of post-truth, this new philosophical concept which originated in the United States, according to which a speech doesn't need to refer to a proven or demonstrated truth, to acknowledge facts, but simply to spur consent and confidence among those who listen. It doesn't matter if what we are saying is true or false; all that matters is that others believe in our *bullshit!*

According to the Washington Post, a very serious report on the CIA examines Russia's influence on fake rumors which were spread around on social networks during the American campaign. What a paradox that

Donald Trump's electors, who seem to herald Pro-American protectionism, were under the indirect influence of a foreign power, especially since this power is the historic rival of their dear country. An additional proof that there is a lot of room for maneuver between the lip service driven by these networks and their hidden intentions.

It's not just the electors or teenagers who don't know how to sort through the information passed around on the Net. Let's recall Kawaja Asif, the Defense Minister of Pakistan who recently threatened Israel for a nuclear response on his Twitter account, after having hastily read a fake information which was broadcasted on an unreliable website.

When one is aware of the compulsive trends of the new American president and his ease of whipping out threats on Twitter, we can't be at peace anymore when it comes to the analytical abilities of those who rule the world. But also, on the consequences.

Anti-social networks-sociopath networks!

The term "social network" is such a malapropism! What is social about having thousands of friends? The "friends" whom we collect on this interface, are they endowed with the benevolence, affection and warmth that the original definition of the term *friendship* is supposed to mean? Or isn't it more about showing off one's ego, as much as possible to people whom we barely know, to build oneself up without giving anything in return? It is just physically impossible to maintain meaningful ties with thousands of people at the same time. This semantic contradiction should be enough to make us understand that the word *friendship*, on these social networks is toned down, voided of all meaning. According to the Law Professor, Roseline Letteron, friendship in terms of the highest jurisdiction possible means: "an intimate acquaintance, closeness, something that a social network can't manage to kindle".

One doesn't find very many friends on social networks; what one finds is a lot of egoism. Andy Warhol had prophesied that every being in the future will have a right to 15 minutes of fame. Did he really think about such low mass consumption? Perhaps yes; after all he reproduced a series of the most mundane objects of everyday life in colored copies. He might have been a visionary, but would he have been frightened to observe all the horror of his prophecy? The dehumanized consequences of each one's capacity of inventing a virtual life?

We like to believe that we are connected with beings whom we've never met, who are at the other end of the globe for some, while we don't even look our own neighbor in the eye. Eyes glued to our screens, exhibiting our lives through a one-way show.

This is such a pity as the electronic media is a wonderful tool to mobilize the masses, for the benefit of righteous causes. It's also a way of staying in touch with real acquaintances, while the circumstances in life took us apart from the latter. We can also find several people through healthy networking who share our sensitivity, refine our areas of expertise with people of the same profession, find a job. Even love, for that matter.

The potential of the Internet tool is just wonderful. The tool isn't the issue here, but the level of conscience with which we use it.

Program our children?

Individualization of our means of communication is not only getting the upper hand on our family units and our way of forging friendships but also on our educational system.

It appears that during every technological revolution, the companies who manufacture state-of-the-art equipment, engage into intense lobbying to urge the National education to buy their latest toys, under the guise of increasing the self-sufficiency of little children and boosting their awareness. There are current talks about providing every French student with a computer screen. But none of the studies show that ICT (Information and communication technology) actually makes a true impact on the development of children. The only certainty is that these young students will get even more used to such kind of tools if their training were to depend on the latter. Is this about deliberately creating an addiction to tablets and computers? It has surely not escaped the attention of Microsoft and consorts that these kids are the consumers of the future.

Let us make no mistake: I am convinced that when a digital tool is properly used, it does have educative values, but it is not a magic bullet, and nothing will be able to replace the connection between the student and the teacher, in the flesh and emotions. As before anything else, we are supposed to train *human beings* and not mere things who absorb whatever is projected in front of them on a screen, like sponges. A computer will never be able to program a human being. Only the opposite remains a possibility.

One can also observe the erosion of the family structure through electronic media at school. All the teachers who were questioned have noticed that the level of impatience has increased during the last decades in students, but also that their expectations about educative tools seems to become increasingly consumerist. This also concerns their parents, accustomed to getting things in a second. They live in the Kleenex era and have lost their sense of contemplation; they don't know the value or the pleasure of discovering things gradually, the autonomous construction of thinking. Like Philippe Bihouix, the co-author of the book *Disaster of Digital school* stated: "in the long run, it's the foundation of the society itself, the conditions of living together, that are questioned".

I could also speak at length about the parents' failure and the increasing number of dysfunctional children. Often these children have very little contact or any kind of true exchange with their parents; their fathers and their mothers, regardless of their social status, are more and more negligent when it comes to an education which leans on the oral tradition, on daily signs of love, which at times doesn't require words but simple gestures like a look or just being present. Alas, parents and children browse alone in their corner and let unknown data dictate nonsense.

Primary classes of today are lagging behind their predecessors, in terms of discipline, attentiveness, benevolence, mutual respect. Moreover, kindergarten teachers say that even little ones already seem to show worrying signs of restlessness and failure to tolerate others. Some infants even portray a certain disgust in terms of physical contact and systematically perceive it as an aggression. Parents of these newborn children come from all kinds of social classes. Rich or poor, they have other things to do rather than educate their children and wish to burden the teachers with their very own failures. A teacher won't be able to replace all these couples who don't know how to love anymore.

Fear on a loop

In dictatorial regimes, propaganda is conveyed through media, in order to convince masses of the supremacy of the official doctrine. But in democracies, we're also able to make an impact through brainwashing messages. Conditioning of minds under an illusionary appearance of diversity is created by a significant number of medias, offered by the West and its fringes, which is quite a dictatorship. What's the point of having so many news channels, if one keeps seeing the same news being repeated throughout the day?

There are distressing reasons due to which media relentlessly keep striking with copied messages in a humdrum tone. Have you noticed, what kinds of feelings are triggered through this kind of news? If only all this had to do with false alarms; but what they sell us is fear. News channels keep broadcasting anxiety-provoking flashes in order to create sensations even when nothing really takes place. They play around with the reptilian part of our brain, basic emotions, the animals that lie within us. Their sensational headlines sell us failure, tragedy, confrontation, breach. Happiness is a much more boring concept, less popular than fear, as it doesn't pay much to the ones who spread it around. Therefore, one doesn't disseminate happiness anymore; one broadcasts the total opposite. Not many journalists even check their sources anymore. What matters is to beat the others to the draw. As long as someone is able to make noise, never mind if the target is missed or if the target doesn't even exist.

This strategy oversteps the boundaries of journalism. Some politicians use this and have turned their jobs into a pure performance. Citizen Kane has got a name in the world today. His name is Donald Trump. When an elected president has the intention of continuing to present the *reality show* which made him popular, even after assuming office, we are dealing with something which goes way beyond absurd. The bounds between show-business and politics have vanished for good. Reality has gone beyond the worst of fictions.

Let's remain measured when it comes to the intentions of powerful men towards Public Affairs, also known as social democracy; but it also depends on the private property of a member or a unique person from a class. Some political figures still try to practice their profession in a dignified manner and for the sake of mutual interest. However, one can lament an underlying trend that gives jitters. Anxiety provoking and nihilistic thoughts, are instilled within us due to some people in charge; their semantics of fear, their verbal violence, their divisive image are brandished to hypnotize us, making us wary of the communities they satirize. These caricatures are no better than any commercial. The foul speeches crystallize hate, bitterness and sourness.

Unfortunately, it's in tune with our times to opt for such a tone. We can even find it in parties who had traditionally turned tolerance into their hobby horse. Evil and non-constructive criticism seems to appear in all areas. *Bashing* and conflation have taken up residence in all the levels of society. One talks about expulsing, purifying, clearing the decks. At times with fire, at least in spirit. One can find Joan of Arcs on every street corner. But sacrificing one's fellowmen doesn't seem to appease anyone. At best, it can lead to bad habits. Such fiery phraseology worries me due to its history. This willingness to clean up, this purification frenzy of fanatical redemption seems to verge on self-destruction. We shall burn in it as well.

A kamikaze rebellion
or a constructive revolution?

Often among us, youth feels lost in this whirlpool, where the bearings are increasingly elusive, a de-sensitized world where lack of recognition ruins them through despair. Some of them are instinctively obsessed by rebellion, due to the youth of their idealism and seem to have found the solution by refuting the system and by rebelling against it.

Rejection of order which has been established, has always been the preserve of the young generation, a sort of irreverence which was often useful, salutary, that brought about renewal in fossilized institutions. Some unworthy youngsters become part of the alter-globalist dance, due to a rejection of this all-pervasive system, which seems to tower everything. For most of them here, one could assume that they mean well due to their utopianism, that they are moved by a thrust of life, an outrage which is a lot like the one of Stephane Hessel. They rebel, hoping to save the world.

Others, on the contrary, enter a religious order as if they were rushing into death. They wish to destroy everything, including their very own lives. These young minds in search of ideals, who lack references, seek a sense of belonging and imprison themselves in a religious fanaticism, rejecting any kind of materialism, rejecting the omnipresence of the West. Their rebellion has no future. Ready to hang onto just anything so that they have the impression of actually existing before dying out, they would even die for a cause that they themselves don't know properly, except for some self-proclaimed religious eminence, who spoon-fed them. The latter are sandmen who in reality are merchants of death under their benevolent simulacrum.

Those who die by dragging others along, claim to do so in the name of a so-called revolution. But in doing so, they don't know the classic sense of this term: *revolvere* in Latin implies a reversal, a disruption, a metamorphosis, a mutation. It implies a future, whatever it may be. Yet the nihilism that is demonstrated by these kamikazes, doesn't promise any future. The passage of youth, the rite of passage to die during childhood has turned into dying, period! It's about destruction, the simple act of destroying; nothing is offered instead of the void they dream to create. Therefore, this isn't about a revolution. Their unrequited approach can't be a culture either. It is the negation itself of the concept of culture. Especially since it is built on nonsense.

Unhooked, based on no values and without any hope on the horizon, these wandering souls have become extremely sensitive to simple, misleading symbols. The shortcuts presented to them, simplifying sacred scriptures at will, distort the original sense of the latter. The ones who manipulate them have taught them to hate but they were careful about not teaching them to read.

The flag of jihads doesn't lean on any historic reality; it only harbors the nostalgia of a fantasized tradition, which is completely out of sync with the past and the true erudite of the Muslim world will be able to demonstrate that it is false.

However, the rebellion of the youth is legitimate with respect to the system's vileness, which refuses to include them. But their way of rejecting the system doesn't hide the awful logic of this same system, as they also have been "convinced" about something which was doctored: a bogus paradise, equally unreliable as these products of bad quality, manufactured at cheap prices by people who are practically slaves whom one can find in the capitalistic world and whose misdemeanors they would like to denounce.

The religious fanatics unknowingly operate according to the mental patterns through which they were conditioned in the society where they were born, even though they seem to reject it, on the surface. Whether they want it or not, they are the products of the system that gave birth to them; they have acquired its official language, even without their own knowledge.

If only these youngsters found out that a human being's awakening to spirituality is a life-time story. One can't brag about having attained enlightenment in such a short span of time, by letting a simple image catch our attention that is vectored by the Internet. Such a sudden enrolment that takes place in two months, or less at times, leading towards a so called promised land, which never existed anywhere except in their fantasies, has nothing to do with a genuine spiritual approach. Regardless of the religion, it is essential to take the time to discover and do some soul searching through meditation, contemplation, reading and the teachings of elders, to achieve a higher state of consciousness. One will never be able to find enlightenment in any supermarket, on any Internet website or *deep web* forum. It'll never be dispatched via Fedex or through a text message. We need to explore ourselves for a long time, before attaining true knowledge.

Current Jihadism conceals angst that is psychological more than ideological. It's both a counter-culture, a kind of nostalgic totalitarianism, ultra-conservative but also extremely individualistic that is a lot like modern marketing. The youngsters who literally fling themselves headlong are scapegoats of the society's disintegration, as if seeking revenge for the humiliation of not being part of things. But a military state, which pretends to be enlightened, connected with the promised paradise in exchange for their sacrifice, in reality only wants to dominate the secular field. The ones who send them out to die in their place have one aim which is to seize power down here. Nothing more nothing less.

Many fighters now wish to go back to their country of origin with their wives and their children, which they wanted to destroy, as they were revolted by the war, the reality on the ground, frightened by the frenzy of their own leaders. Perhaps this is the beginning of redemption for them, perhaps they needed to go through this horror of killing to really feel revolted. Maybe they could improve themselves, if they learned from their own mistakes and we gave them a chance to do so.

Everyone will need to express a great amount of love to undo the evil. It'll be difficult to circumvent all the bloodshed, but this shouldn't be impossible.

Unity Is Strength

Throughout history, it turns out that events revolving around tolerance, the pooling of talents and convivence outbursts, meant the same as taking steps, progressing, increasing knowledge and feeling fulfilled for the people who were concerned.

Going back to the prehistoric times yields valuable insights. Even if what we know today about the functioning of the prehistoric societies can be analyzed in various ways, at times contradictory, evidence suggests that *Homo sapiens* hunters were more capable of ensuring the survival of their tribes when they began hunting in groups, especially during the Ice Age when it was difficult to find a prey and its size was way too heavy for a single hunter to knock it down.

It has also been recognized that 30,000 years ago, when the life expectancy of human beings increased in such a way that a majority between them could witness the birth of their grandchildren (to put it otherwise, when the life expectancy surpassed 35 years of age), the development of human community sped up in a spectacular manner. Indeed, grandparents passed on their experience to their descendants, in terms of social rules, know-how but also triggered reflexes of mutual help. The fact that these forebears were available to take care of the upbringing of young children, allowed the parents to devote themselves to tasks that only they could tackle. Adults in the prime of life had more time to hunt or gather resources, which were necessary for the tribe's life. They also had the luxury to devote themselves to more creative and intellectual activities rather than just simple survival. This is how an unprecedented progress of arts and craftsmanship for *Homo sapiens* coincided with the key date of 30,000 years before our own era. The emergence of grandparents represented a certain advantage from the viewpoint of evolution but also a precious societal bond. The symbiosis of generations helped strengthen social ties, density of populations, their productivity and inventiveness. This righteous spiral, dating back to thirty thousand years ago, was the origin of a population density that created the first urban centers and the emergence of civilizations that was our cradle. It was the initial spark that led towards cultural and commercial development of which we still benefit today.

This is a contrasting comparison with the way we now marginalize the elderly as useless rejects: it often happens that we confine the elderly in a hospice where they can't pass on anything to anyone. By dint of dismissing them, through the excuse that they won't be productive anymore or that their physical appearance isn't in keeping with the criteria of beauty of the times, once again highlights our superficiality and our cultural impoverishment. We'll get the chance to talk about old generations to structure the society, pass on knowledge and fight against ignorance. Convivence needs to be inter-generational as well.

Coming back to the prehistoric era, even though we still don't really know how well *Homo sapiens* cooperated with the Neanderthal man, even if their common history was certainly made up of alternating periods which involved conflicts and more cooperative times, genetics has demonstrated that we still have traces of interbreeding, in our very own DNA and therefore a form of convivence between these two species.

Beyond our genes, paleontology suggests that our spirituality still supports concepts which would have been passed on from our cousin, who is now defunct: it appears to be plausible that the latter taught us to bury our dead and decorate our tombs with objects intended to accompany the deceased in their next life. The fact that we even envisage life after death, considered as the nature of humanity by some, could be a legacy. At least, this is what Yves Coppens strongly states in the documentaries *L'Odyssée de l'espèce* and *Homo*

Sapiens: this spiritual heritage allowed *Homo sapiens* to become what is today known as the social animal, equipped with a higher level of conscience. If we were capable of sharing our beliefs with other hominid species, why would we be incapable of tolerating our own blood brothers?

In addition, it is possible that the Neanderthal man disappeared due to his major sedentary lifestyle compared to the one of *Sapiens*, who travelled more, exchanged with many more cultures and showed the great capacity of enriching himself through foreign contribution. Other adaptability factors to a changing environment should certainly be considered, when it comes to the disappearance of the Neanderthal man; but *Homo Sapiens* slowly got the upper hand over the Neanderthal by diversifying his cultural relations in a more efficient manner but also by thriving. The beneficial aspects of the capacity to collaborate, to be curious about others, are highlighted further.

Our common experiences

Let's flash back to tens of thousands of years ago and then move forward to our very own era. Even if it is known as the "Christian era", it always involves the advent of other religions which are second to none with Christianity in terms of popularity.

Given the current atmosphere, who still remembers the way Islam and Judaism peacefully cohabitated for almost 1,500 years? Who still remembers that these two religions that we now oppose in a Manichean manner, came into being through mutual exchange, through constant and fruitful interactions, whose teachings they still retain?

The notion of *clash of civilizations* that we currently try to disseminate within minds, culture of fear and the blood one promotes, is the same as *clash of ignorance* which hides the will to fracture communities. Divide to rule.

Faced with this decline, confronted with reductive stereotypes that hover around our skies, we have a duty of remembrance. We won't be able to list out everything that we are trying to forget, but it's urgent to set out certain avenues that each one will be free to intensify through a more personal approach. Can we still remember that the ancient links between Islam and Judaism touched religion, philosophy, arts, architecture, science, culinary arts and several practices of daily life? In fact, Arab and Hebrew are both Semitic languages which have several points in common. The respective religious practices of these two religions were subject to exchanges, productive confrontations, textual exegesis, works of men who didn't share the other's faith but tried to understand its teachings. Indeed, according to me it is important to keep in mind that all religions talk about the same thing, even social codes and traditions which they incorporate, despite the images and parables each one uses to pass on its message through changing colors and appearance. It's the brotherly love which is inherent in every belief. This is what is essential. The late poet Abdelwahab Medeb summed this up better than anybody else: "Ultimately, all human beings have one and the same religion, whose expressions and ceremonies differ".

This passing on of knowledge, these mutual exchanges couldn't have taken place if these two communities constantly tried to kill or hate each other or had remained abstruse to one another through a fantasized isolation.

Within a framework of reflection, the historic example of al-Andalus is essential because it spawned the term, which we wish to revitalize, the one of *Convivencia.*

Everything wasn't idyllic between the Muslim, Sephardic Jewish and Visigoth communities during this long experience which was centered around Andalusia between the 7th and 12th century, but which stretched out from Spain till Provence. However, it is undeniable that those peoples who were so different, traded, exchanged knowledge, even married one another during this period, in a relatively peaceful atmosphere and for the purpose of justice and respect for the other. It was also a prolific period which was the cradle of the current Jewish cultural identity and left three distinct civilizations who were enriched from the teachings of the two others. This for example, allowed the historian Eliyahu Ashtor to state that al-Andalus saw "Jewish history [...] go through its most flourishing period-the one which led to an exceptional influence on the destiny of the Jews and Judaism".

After the Arabs conquered Andalusia during the 7th century, each one in al-Andalus was able to freely practice their religion and preserve their place of worship. Artists, scientists, the religious and Jewish doctors cooperated with Muslim scientists and philosophers. The Arab civilization had already made a great step forward in terms of the medieval obscurantism which stifled the European Christian, who benefited as much. Arab philosophy (*al falsafa)* came into existence during this period, while the Arab scholars devoted themselves to major works of translation in Greek philosophy, especially Aristotle.

The most representative symbol of this interbreeding is Moshe ibn Maymun, best known under the name Maimonide, a Jewish philosopher from the 12th century whose works inspired this revitalized Arab thinking and influenced three different religions (Judaism, Islam and Christianity) not only in their philosophic approach but spiritual and juridical as well. The writings of Maimonide are an eloquent illustration of the mutual influences of communities on one another within the Andalusian context.

Therefore, the Jews found a new impetus in this intellectual turbulence. *Al falsafa* was key for the creation of Jewish philosophy as for the Muslim theory (*Kalam), which* inspired more than one Jewish thinker. Moreover, it's through practicing and studying the official Arab language that the Sephardic revealed a fruitful revival on their own language. For the first time in their history, Jewish linguists had a scientific approach towards Hebrew, which then turned into "a way of structured and reasoned expression" according to the ethnographer, Shelomo Dov Goitein. Through extending, the Hebrew poetry came across an unprecedented and renewed effervescence under the impetus of this research and the power of Arab literature. Goitein concludes: "Hebrew poetry in Spain was the product of the Muslim civilization".

On a more secular level, it was also during this period that the Jews practiced professional activities other than soil cultivation, something to which they were traditionally devoted until that time. They became bankers, traders, artisans… Some even became political advisors to sultans, the ultimate sign of open-mindedness and trust on behalf of Muslim leaders in other communities who shared their territory. It was also the Andalusian Sephardic who passed down scientific enlightenment of the Arab civilization to the Christian West.

One of the most sensational cultural relics of this golden age and virtuous circle, which supported these communities, lies in the Arab-Andalusian musical heritage. The result of the Eastern, Arab, Berber, Andalusian traditions, Arab-Andalusian music was that it influenced musicians in their compositions and instruments throughout the Mediterranean basin, right up to Christian Europe.

There is so much to say on the relations between Islam and Judaism. One could speak at length about tolerance, regarding the Sephardic in the Ottoman Empire around 13th century, a gentle submission policy from Muslim sovereigns, surely more pragmatic than Judeophile, but not less intelligent as they knew the necessity of using talents of each one of them, so that the society could prosper. Mainly the city of Thessaloniki, which reaped the benefits by welcoming Jews who had been evicted from the Iberian Peninsula after the collapse of al-Andalus at the hands of Christians. Letting the Jews practice all kinds of professions without any restriction what-soever turned this harbor city into a leading commercial and cultural hub. The Jews flour-ished due to this foundation; however at the same time, other Jewish communities who had taken refuge elsewhere in the world were persecuted, tormented and slaughtered.

The same goes for the long existence of Jews in Morocco, where the Judeo-Muslim collabo-ration was particularly rich and prolific, despite the fact that the national identity asserted itself only at the end of 15th century. Moreover, the last Moroccan constitution thus far defines and accepts the cultural plurality of this country. It is explicitly stated that the Arab-Islamic identity comes from a historic reality, irrigated by the Andalusians, entire Africa, the Berber culture, Judaism… It is asserted that Morocco today, which is an Arab and Muslim society, was coined by the chronological addition of several cultures. This text represents the fundamentals of a promising social, political, spiritual and cultural modernity. Perhaps France should draw inspiration from the fact that one can accept a national identity with several origins?

Beyond their genuine differences, the two religious traditions of Islam and Judaism were partially shaped through the encounter with the other. It's only with the incursion of Europeans in the East and in North Africa from 19th century onwards, that the Jewish communities began to distance themselves from Muslims, with whom they had already been in good terms in the past. Countering Judaism and Islam in the short term, as if their relationships had always been conflictual, as if it had always been the case, seems completely absurd. Although this is what several speeches and theories try and make us believe since the beginning of the 20th century. Be it only in Palestine.

Contrary to the acceptance of the official speeches, the Israeli-Palestinian conflicts aren't a religious conflict per se, as it is the result of the confrontation of two national movements: Zionism and Arab-Palestinian nationalism. Both of these two very recent movements, in regard to history, aspire to their political sovereignty in Palestine. But these minds that see themselves as enemies have re-invented and distorted the respective identities of their communities, which they pretend to represent by including religion in their ideological arguments with the sole aim of justifying their territorial claims. Religion, which is supposed to be a founding bond of the nation has turned into an excluding tool that is manipulated by two radical groups, who have sanctified a land and, through selective reinterpretation of holy scriptures, have built up a belief against the others, all the while considering themselves to be rightfully superior. As long as the parties here refuse to review this spiritual dishonesty, this situation will lead to nothing but a simple and vain dialogue of the deaf and no good will come out of this.

Teachings of Buddhism

Buddhism, from our European viewpoint could culturally seem more distant in terms of the three of monotheistic religions. But some of the Buddhist doctrine teachings have already inspired a generation of Western philosophers, mainly Germanic: Goethe, Thomas Mann and Hermann Hesse, right on the top. The latter, already disillusioned by Western materialism as from the beginning of the industrial revolution, turned towards the Eastern enlightenment, to find peace of mind.

Buddhism was founded twenty-five centuries ago; it is both an arcane philosophy and a moral framework. Some countries like Bhutan have made it their official religion. Harmonious and inter-generational cohabitation, sharing capacities of each one in favor of the community are its building blocks, to such an extent that the king of Bhutan, Jigme Singye Wangchuck, established the notion of the *gross national happiness,* displaying a clear desire of putting the well-being of his citizens before economic growth. The current Prime Minister Tsering Tobgay underlines: "If one needs to think about a project which favors economic development, only one question can guide us: will it make us happier? Of course, richer… but happier?"

Just like the Buddhist Theravada doctrine, the outcome of the oldest Buddhist school (Sthaviravada), which mainly influences Burma, Laos and Cambodia, pervades the aspects of everyday life in these countries. According to this school of thought, our good deeds will lead to positive consequences in our future incarnations. Whether we believe in reincarnation or not, this doctrine's main principle namely unity is strength, highlights community strength and encourages people to interact with respect and has direct measurable consequences on our current incarnations. The rituals, which give rhythm to the lives of these believers, give the opportunity to gain merits or ask the higher powers to intervene. Merit (*punya* in Sanskrit) originates from good thoughts or any good deed and contributes to the spiritual liberation and of "living together". The importance that is given to the moral teachings of Theravada Buddhism in families largely explains the extremely benevolent manner with which citizens lead their lives and an expression of genuine solidarity with one another. In Burma, the traveler is astonished by the civility with which the Burmese treat visitors.

It is also due to an altruistic intention that king Anawratha, a believer of the Theravada doctrine strived to unify the Burmese nation during the 11th century, by making sure to include all the ethnicities in the national project. It was the latter who came back with some 30,000 prisoners during his conquests, to unify the four main kingdoms and smartly used their talents to build magnificent monasteries and pagodas which we can still find in this country. An additional proof which encourages the fact that living together helps to sow-and reap-prosperity.

Foundation for the future

Once we have established that we are sick with egoism and once the historical proof has been given that convivence is feasible, where do we go from here?

A transformation in our lifestyles seems to be essential. A paradigm shift. A "reversal", if we were to refer to the etymology of the word revolution (revolvere). Destruction might be useful if it can lead to a renewal, according to the creative destruction concept, established by the economist Joseph Schumpeter: "Novelty doesn't come from the old, but it appears next to the old, competing against it until it is ruined". An elegant way of saying that one can't make a fresh start with the old. But we also need to accept what needs to be recognized as "old". If old is synonymous with what doesn't work anymore, something which is obsolete in regard to the evolution of societies and customs, it is assured that fresh blood, innovative ideas are a must. Perhaps one might need to look for this renewal in certain values that we have forgotten, and which deserve to be highlighted. Tossing away all the teachings of the past in an indiscriminate manner, will be way too close to nihilism for it to be beneficial.

The idea of convivence needs to re-adapt itself to the modern era. We are no longer in Andalusia of the 7th century, during our era. We live in a global village. In this way, the anthropologist Marc Abeles explains that convivence during the political speeches of the 20th century represented a notion of "being together" which was included in the framework of the Nation states. The latter now prefers to substitute a concept of survival confronted with globalization issues and the elimination of national borders as it would make more sense following the emergence of what one could appropriately call the "international civil society". Indeed, the stakes have been globalized: they include factors that prevent from examining the cultural features of a precise community: a foundation, isolated from others. As for the interconnection of communication networks, the dominant position now revolves around areas like ecology, climate, sustainable development, challenges that are faced by the entire Humanity, which also needs to be considered when it comes to our relations with the other. Societies are more culturally diverse compared to before and due to the emergence of the global means of communication; our capacity to know and interact with Humanity in all its diversity makes up a true cultural revolution for the new generation.

To regulate our exchanges with other cultures, taking a sort of "International civic virtue" appears to be necessary. Without glorifying an ideology or something else, we can indeed consider this to be an International form, in the proper sense of the word. We aren't talking about class warfare but a collaboration. A collaboration across species, regardless of authority, customs, traditions or each one's history.

Sovereignty has shifted, understanding our environment has broadened. Convivence needs to adapt to these factors which have recently appeared. Today, we need to apprehend within a global framework.

Environmental Convivence

For this purpose, it seems to be important to include the non-human in the system of modern convivence. It is the same lack of altruism as the one which divides human communities, the same ignorance which pushes some of us to neglect the consequences of our egoistic action in terms of the environment. Through negligence, pursuit of profit, saving time, we carry out destructive actions over the planet and we don't seem to understand the consequences, as they're rarely visible in a direct and immediate manner. We forget that by not taking care of our surroundings, we are jeopardizing our very own survival.

"When the last tree will be cut down, the last river shall be poisoned, the last fish will be fished, you'll discover that one can't eat money". This American proverb isn't new, it dates back to the beginning of the industrial era. However, it takes into account the scarcity of natural resources and climatic changes, worrisome prophesies of the current situation.

The desire to backtrack on certain climatic agreements, which are already too weak and superficial, even late, shows the unhealthy sense of priorities of some obsessed decision-makers due to monetary compensation.

However, these environmental stakes transcend the community and national context.

Certainly, there is a lot to discuss around jobs that could create a real commitment towards a more sustainable economy rather than consumerism, something on which we don't wish to give up. However, solutions still exist. We still need to take them into consideration.

Let's simply quote Gaël Giraud, an economist at the French Development agency, to illustrate the challenges and opportunity. According to the latter, one must move forward quickly "[...] towards a post-carbon economy. The project is a job creator and a bearer of meaning and social ties, as it has a political dimension which is collective and positive. In short, it revives this 'desire for the future' which is key for the balance of any society [...]".

***

Whether we still use the term *convivence* or we replace it by something else, doesn't really matter. It's the substance of the chosen term and its adaptation to our modernity that matters, as its relevance and efficiency depends on it. This is perfectly expressed by Michel

Maille, from the faculty of Law at Montpellier in *Citizenship and Convivence:*

> "Of course, things are far from being as simple for the definition of these fundamental principles and therefore the values that make up the 'sanctity of the social contract' are never given in advance. It varies from one century to another, depending on our contradictions, its conflicts and the issues that are encountered. It is part of all principles and social orders. Therefore, each generation is responsible for the convivence that it defines and implements".

Upon which path should we embark in order to renew our social contract? We don't have the pretension to draw out a complete list or provide ready-made solutions to such a complex problem, but it seems important to point out some pitfalls and define some lines of thought which we encourage each one to enrich, contradict in a constructive manner and nourish through experience and knowledge.

Resume faith in secularism

A founding pillar of our Republic, secularity is a poorly understood notion by the French and is often misused. Do we actually know what it precisely means? We won't be able to discourse on it better than Lucien Jaume, whose article in the journal *Commentaire,* concerning Jules Ferry's thought is a clear and pertinent model. His approach is based on the fact that, when it comes to secularity for the French (mainly in the field of the education system), it is synonymous with the founding education laws from 1881 till 1882 and the one separating state and religion in 1905. However, the latter underlines the opposite side of the misconceptions: the legislation of 1905 doesn't mention the term *secularity.* This confusion unveils a shift in meaning, even of secularity in terms of public awareness. Have we turned secularity into a false prospectus, which might have drifted away from the initial submission, like others might have misread their gospel and turned them into excluding and oppressing instruments? Can someone secular be capable of misguided ways, misinterpretation and psychological inflexibility, just like an Ultra-Orthodox sectarian? Are the representatives of the Republic, knowingly or not, capable of blind fundamentalism? Or do they think they that they are as unerring as the fanatics against whom they claim to stand?

According to Lucien Jaume, the religious wasn't missing in Jules Ferry's philosophy and philosophers of the French Revolution, who were inspired by this approach. When it came to these enlightened minds, who were most of all concerned about mending the Nation after the revolutionary division which had caused bloodshed in our country, "one rediscovers the search of a connection between the political and the sectarian, that ensures the social order, which [turns] the citizen into a renewed being [...] and obtains a collective identity whose key is possessed by the Nation and State. Concerned about restoring national cohesion after a period of division and tension, which sadly culminated during the famous episode of the Commune, Jules Ferry never spoke about a *secular moral* but a *secular education*. According to the latter, moral is unique: therefore, it can't be the prerogative of a section of society or a school of thought, nor a doctrine. Moreover, Jules Ferry recognizes the religious contribution in the construction of a *universal* moral: the latter maintained that "moral secular education is different from religious teaching, without contradicting it".

Ferry wanted to pacify consciences, unite the nation through its diversity and claimed the "desire of an anticlerical struggle but never a religious struggle" and warned us against "irreligious fanatism [...] which is as bad as the first one".

Didn't Victor Cousin who inspired Jules Ferry say that a secular State "isn't indifferent or atheist; but mainly moral and religious, as the idea of justice on which it has been founded is holy and sacred". Julies Ferry wholeheartedly agreed by saying that the curricula of the Republic, were *spiritualists,* "because a vast majority of the French population sticks to spiritualist beliefs".

Therefore, we are far from the *secularity* that many of us seem to define. This wasn't about Ferry dividing or excluding or even imposing a sterile uniqueness, through standardizing and forbidding others to believe in their faith within the public realm; it was about bringing together and endorsing our values on a common core, resulting from several contributions. It was about building a Republican moral, by using religious and family bases where the "fundamental notions of eternal and universal moral" lies.

Today, understanding secularity once again creates debates in an almost systematic manner. When we see that Manuel Valls, the former Prime Minister is himself opposed to the Observatory on secularism (though part of Matignon), on the definition of the term itself, when we see that the regulations in terms of ostentatious religious signs are scalable as they vary between schools, universities, work places and public spaces and thus betray a kind of uncertainty, hesitation or even bad faith, it would be commendable to finally have "a real debate" on the substance and the purpose of secularity, just like Nicolas Cadene, reporter of the same Observatory, would like to.

The European Institute in sciences of religions (IESR) points out that Philippe Joutard in 1989 and Régis Debray in 2002, "expressed support for the necessity of teaching religious facts in a secular school. [...]

Religious facts are sociological and cultural facts which have put down roots in history, geography and humanities… Therefore, they should be included in the impartial teaching of these disciplines. It isn't about catechesis but knowledge".

To put it otherwise, two acceptations of the term *secularity* are opposed in France: one is open and inclusive and the other is combative and restrictive. On one hand, atheists who wish to appropriate the apanage of secularism; on the other, more open minds, along the lines of Jean-Louis Bianco who stated: "Those who distort secularity, are precisely those who make of it an anti-religious, anti-Muslim tool and who argue (which is a monumental mistake when it comes to the principal of secularity itself) that the public space is completely neutral, as if we didn't even have the right to our opinions anymore".

It goes without saying that the notion of convivence has become part of this open acceptation of secularity, urging to interpret the notion of tolerating a range of various tendencies. Debates around the burkini, regardless of what one might think about this clothing, are an insult to the notion of secularity and the ones who agree with this are still willing to debate on this issue.

As long as the Republic won't be heard on the substance of its founding values, as long as the representatives won't be consistent and rational with what they have to say, it'll be impossible to promote and make all the citizens accept these founding values. The risk of fracture between the communities that make it up, shall be worsened. If so many of our citizens are outraged and reject the institutions indiscriminately, withdraw on themselves, through communitarian and intolerant reflexes, it is also because they feel that they are the victims of intolerance, tormented for their beliefs and their dreams and for the sharp speeches of those who represent them

The collective unconscious of the nation is certainly blackened with a form of spiritual castration; the rejection of certain fundamental bearings has ruined the balance of psyches. The distinguished psychoanalyst, Carl Jung was already worried about the deconstruction of a certain mysticism, at the beginning of the 20th century: "By demolishing Olympus, we have turned Gods into symptoms".

Let's take this reflection beyond the religious aspect, let's consider the stakes of this debate on secularity. Following the example of other values of the Republic which deserve to be examined as well, secularity has its role in the construction of a political project, a vision for the future of the nation, depending on the way we accept the latter. As Gaël Giraud points out, "no society can live without a great narrative, in a way reminiscent of the ones who make it up, why they live together and what kind of future they wish to pass on to their children". However, according to the latter,

France has become an "orphan in terms of a vision" since about forty years. A societal flaw seems to emerge because there is no collective dream. It's our entire founding myth that needs to be rejuvenated, in which we need to have faith and consider ourselves as a united society, capable of welcoming our sons and daughters within all beliefs and aspirations, without any exception. A blatant lack of verticality has severed the capacity of many of our citizens to treat us as a united entity, but it has also jeopardized the respect of our social contract. The aim of convivence would be to revive this passion of living together, this faith we share for a common destiny.

May France be named diversity
(F. Braudel)

Fantasizing about an original, pure and genuine society is an illusion in which each community has the habit of wallowing. Thinking that a culture (in the collective sense of the term) is an unchanging and non-progressive object, integrally casted into a stone is an illusion. Of course, culture of the people can seem to be steadfast over a lifetime, as its evolution is often slower than the culture in the individual sense of its acceptation (namely the entire knowledge of a given individual) and therefore more difficult to perceive. Of course, culture of the people is characterized through a set of values which have roots in the past and are a reminder when it comes to the History of a community. But the fact remains that the culture of a community is built up through conflation, through a slow sedimentation of outside sources which nourish and transform it. Otherwise, we would still be speaking Rabelaisian French in France.

Theories that study cross-cultural phenomenon entirely agree with this. According to Claude Clanet, a former professor in social science at Toulouse University, the term *intercultural* introduces notions of reciprocity, when it comes to exchanges and complexity in relations between cultures. These interactions between individuals that are a result of various cultures, generate a new cultural code in the long run, as a result of progressive interbreeding, in the development of a new social model which is better adapted to everyone and each one, allowing to surpass the differences. The open approach of cultural integration in terms of customs and traditions of the other is opposed to ethnocentrism, that the computerized *Treasure of the French language* defines as a "social behavior and an attitude, which is subconsciously motivated and therefore favors and overestimates a racial, geographic or national group to which we belong, at times leading to preconceptions with respect to other people".

Through its colonial history, the waves of immigration mainly during the 20th century, French society is today made up of people who are natives from all continents and faiths: Catholicism, Judaism, Protestantism, Islam, Hinduism, Buddhism... not to mention regional cultures which are still perennial, as in Corsica or Brittany. This plural vision of our Republic has already been supported by the historian, Fernand Braudel in *Identity of France: "May France be named diversity!"*, he proclaimed.

It is up to us to reacquire all that beauty and potential but also to adapt convivence to the reality of our plural and progressive society. Let us make no mistake, including various external sources that have made us the France of today, has never taken place without periods of adjustment or even conflicts for that matter. The world is made up of exchanges that are more or less violent or friendly; it has always been this way. But isolationism has never led to anything but decline, not to mention cultural, spiritual, genetic and economic impoverishment.

Equality in touch with convivence

Growing inequality has come into being due to some people who are able to build on their wealth and this certainly seems to make an impact on the growth of social division, which itself triggers tensions between the various strata of modern society. When inequality is perceived as an injustice, it can only fire up violence and division, thus be detrimental to convivence. But of course, we can understand that empty bellies have the tendency of easily leaning on extreme and cleaving discussions, compared to those who are provided with shelter, food and a place to live. How can someone who lives below the poverty line not feel resentment or jealousy towards *celebrities,* whose charmed lives are displayed by the media, portraying their material predominance as something completely inaccessible? In such a position, who wouldn't feel the desire to destroy those who wave around abundance in full sight of someone who is deprived of the latter?

In this way, James Pool demonstrated in his book *Who Financed Hitler,* that the rise of Nazism and Communism in the Weimar Germany was promoted through the extreme poverty of the German population. The "wealthy Jewish" easily became responsible for the misfortunes of Germans, a foul beast who suck the lifeblood out of the *Fatherland* and therefore needed to be eliminated, urgently.

Gilles Keppel in *Revenge of God* established the fact that the rise of the Islamic salvation Front in Algeria during the 90's, was favored by the failure of the Algerian state in the poor areas of this country. The ISF replaced the government, serving as the alternative social structure and "taking advantage of a disillusionment, in regard to secular ideologies and utopias, of a general distress".

Regarding our own time and country, the sociologist Said Bouamama blames some promoting speeches of "living together", for instilling a sort of naive optimism and not heading towards the heart of the issue, by neglecting the deterioration of material reality in their reasoning, which afflicts "sensitive neighborhoods", where communitarism seems to thrive more easily:

"These problems are related to three procedures studied in other writings: a process of massive impoverishment, generalized insecurity and racial discrimination touching all scarce goods (housing, employment, etc.). The consensual speech of 'living together' therefore hides the reality of increasing inequalities which destroy the life of the lower classes generally speaking and the one of their constituent parts, an outcome of the post-colonial immigration in particular".

Deeply rooted convivence in fact, will therefore be achieved by revising the sharing of resources not only because they are more and more limited and that our model of excessive consumption is a headlong pursuit that has reached its limit and can't keep taking advantage of the planet as it has always been doing, but also because the social inequalities are the obvious reasons for the gap, which has led to resentment. According to Gaël Giraud, one will need to "review our relationship with private property, a man-thing relationship in which we have trapped ourselves since the.... Roman Empire!"

For all that, does the ideal of a society based on convivence require equality among all the citizens? Of course not. As it has been pointed out by John Rawls and Amartya, some inequalities are fair and beneficial when they exist for the advantage of the less fortunate. Convivence requires respecting differences, these include difference in class, social status and wealth-provided that these differences aren't perceived as a flagrant injustice and help the most disadvantaged to progress up the social ladder, to their will.

A new reflection on our society, on our social contract, on property and our national identity is a must. These revamped and readapted values to contemporary realities could unite the society and turn into a strong sign of a new-found willingness to integrate but could also be a solid guarantee for peace among citizens, wherever they come from, in accordance with their plurality and their freedom of conscience. A clear and coordinated definition of these values will help overcome the obstacles of globalization, communitarianism and rejection trends, which the drastic evolution that the global society seems to be currently generating.

Brotherhood's ability to listen

In order to agree on the founding principles of our common dream, in order to be able to establish all its terms one needs to be capable of instituting genuine dialogue. The form of dialogue remains to be defined but it is already a certainty that it needs to be carried out on all levels of the society (whether it concerns family, State, enterprise, school…) and include all the components. It is also required to respect some rules that will guarantee that this dialogue shall be rich and the bearer of solutions. But what does dialogue mean, in the true sense of the term?

Its Greek root *dia-logos* shall be translated through a confrontation of distinct logics. By broadening, dialogue requires a reasoned and effective remark which penetrates, judges but also completely and meticulously springs ideas to mind, through the aim of convincing the interlocutor. Genuine dialogue also involves mutual respect from all the participants, the capacity to put oneself in other people's shoes and understand the viewpoint of each and every person. It is about building up a discourse, coming up with a solution to a problem together, while each one provides their share of arguments and tries to converge them with the ones of others, rather than oppose them. For this, one needs to be wise and lean on judgment and reason. But without being right *compared* to the other one and even less, trying to *get the upper hand* on the other person.

This is how dialogue calls upon those who are willing to be attentive and show humility. According to an African saying "genuine dialogue requires recognition of the other, in terms of integrity and alterity". We see that genuine dialogue seems to make complete sense, within a framework of convivence as it calls upon the same values and qualities of listening, sharing but also conciliation. It's about combining our freedom, our notions of justice, dignities, our love, our symbolism and our dreams, to find a common area for our alterities. Genuine dialogue is the foundation on which conviction can be built. In fact, this was the ethical message of discussion, developed by the philosopher Jurgen Habermas.

With respect to humility, in order for a discourse to be constructive, it is important to take the subjectivity of our perceptions into account. We all take action; we are all able to perceive, depending on our filters, fears and aspirations. The neuroscientists and other psychologists consider "cognitive biases" as blinkers, which prevent us from listening or understanding the truth. Moreover, difficulties of pronouncement do exist, that are specific to a speaker who might have a hard time expressing himself, speaking clearly and getting through. This difficulty could lead to several misunderstandings and confusion. Due to all these reasons, it often happens that we hear something completely different from what the other person is trying to explain.

But no misunderstandings seem insurmountable for anyone who wants to keep in mind that our humanity makes us all capable of possessing the same feelings, the best and the worst ones. We can all commit the bad, spread hate and violence, in the same way as we can show compassion, love and be self-giving.

Therefore, it'll be completely absurd to believe that only others are capable of intolerance and reprehensible actions. Shifting the blame of intolerance and the source of evil on the other person is already an exclusion reflex and therefore sows the seeds of intolerance.

This has been underlined by two specialists of organizational theories, Carl Cederstrom and André Spicer, in their joint publication called *The Syndrome of Well-Being*: "in order to put up with the burden of our failures, faced with our disability to respond to the expectations of wellbeing, it seems to be easier to blame others".

Along similar lines, it seems impossible to try and establish a hierarchy between the various sufferings that have been over-whelming one or the other throughout History. It cannot be said that the slavery suffered by the ancestors of Afro-American, or the Shoah, or the Armenian genocide or the massacres of Rwanda are worthy of more compassion than other human tragedies. Treating one's own sufferings, as an ethnicity, population or religion, as being more serious than the one of others, creates already an area of discord. Believing that one's sufferings is more painful than the other, worthier of more revenge or resentment, is already positioning oneself as the victim, a martyr, or appropriating a right of superiority over one's brothers. This opens floodgates to all kinds of fanaticisms.

We are all equal in the presence of suffer-ings and joys, dreams and nightmares, in the presence of our capacity of doing the right or the wrong. This common trait should bring us together and not divide us. Treating oneself as an exception, is like giving up on the idea of reconstituting oneself and allowing oneself all the mistakes, without taking responsibility.

Without any responsibility-that is to say without accepting one's responsibility that we are all responsible for our very own remarks, facts and actions, not to mention beliefs-we don't leave any room for convivence.

Political Correctness made in France

To ensure that a dialogue is constructive, the aim is therefore to let the other one speak freely. It is also about naming the evil so that one is able to identify but also counter it. However, several scholars in France deplore a sort of vigilance, conformism, intimidation, a new form of censorship, even self-censorship for that matter, when some taboo topics are addressed. Talking about issues related to integration in the suburbs, racism, identity crisis affecting some of our citizens, lifting the weight of the colonial legacy on the French immigration is often poorly perceived just like talking about Vichy's France or the Dreyfus affair.

Pascal Blanchard, the historian, is among those who have denounced the lack of debate in these areas, mainly when it comes to the political parties whether it's the left or the right wing. The latter holds the French elite responsible for burying their head into the sand regarding these issues, and for finding drastic and dead-end solutions.

Michel Onfray, the philosopher, considers it to be injurious that these same parties take refuge in some kind of denial, when faced with these issues. The latter regrets that only the extreme right can address some realities which seem to touch the daily lives of the French. By doing so, he doesn't apologize for these extreme thoughts; but deplores a monopoly when it comes to reality and only observes the resignation of these historical parties in the matter, whereas they are the ones who should shoulder their responsibilities, not to mention to be in the limelight.

When extreme philosophers blatantly express themselves, the most nuanced ones have a hard time talking: the latters consider themselves to be victims of a certain kind of deafness when they try to point out sensitive questions. This is when they perceive a hostile reaction, a general outcry as if they were violating a law of correct-thinking. We caricature those who have the audacity to offer alternatives and we immediately accuse them of Neo-racism, anti-Semitism or other unworthy names. A kind of French *political correctness* converts the one who exposes himself as someone promoting unhealthy ideas, which need to be denounced.

Laurent Martin, the historian, calls this "*soft* totalitarianism". Or the philosopher Laurent Fides says: "Some journalists and philosophers are specialized in the art of unmasking deviants and identifying pathologies of non-compliant thinking. […] Instead of responding to arguments by other arguments, they consider the remarks to be symptoms".

This easy way out-turning the messenger into a scapegoat-allows to dispose of sensitive questions without actually dealing with them, keeping them under wraps until the next time. This method results in breaking off dialogue, refusing to debate when it's necessary. But burying one's head in the sand in the long run cannot outlast. Reality will one day or another, catch up with those who are in denial. If the philosophers don't commit to questions which create the fear of other, there won't be any way out.

One shouldn't be scared of debating and should always keep in mind that freedom of expression is essential in France just like anywhere else. George Orwell already prophesized this at the beginning of the 20th century: "Speaking of freedom doesn't make sense, unless it's the freedom of telling people those things they don't wish to hear".

If mistakes have been made, if political decisions partly led to divisions, which seem to cloud us, one will need to acknowledge these, in order to give ourselves the chance to change directions. Living together admits this refusal of *politically correct* as the *sine qua non* condition: listening, soul searching, rooting out the evil, accepting mistakes, learning and growing.

"To set oneself free is also to seek freedom for others" (Simone de Beauvoir)

According to Robert Maggiori, in his book called *De la Convivance,* one of the peculiar principles of our contemporaries is the inability to make a choice. Each one seems to wallow in hesitation, to claim an illusion of freedom. However, the philosopher explains that this difficulty of taking responsibility for one's decisions cancels all attempts towards convivence. Indeed, convivence requires the possibility to uphold the will of the other over one's own, to choose what the other one desires and what is beneficial to many, over one's own. Surpassing one's ego, this philosophy of love is a *sine qua non* condition in terms of convivence: one can get a taste of happiness only by sharing it.

Alain Romero, mayor of Espondeilhan, expresses the same idea in other terms:

> "Convivence isn't a law enshrined in various codes [...] It isn't imprinted in books, but it asks every individual to be capable of his or her own

self-sufficiency, be responsible and reasonable, respectful of oneself and others, be a secular disciple of mutual tolerance".

Hence the legitimate question: Does convivence lean on the altruism of individuals? Better: what part of altruism do we need to enforce in order to ensure harmonious human relations?

A broad topic: the one of the effects of an altruistic attitude, which is treated pertinently in the writings of Matthieu Ricard, mainly in his book called *Plaidoyer pour l'altruisme (Plea for altruism)*. Matthieu Ricard develops aplenty of arguments, scientific and historical examples, proving that the beneficial strength of living together is part of reality. He supports the fact that benevolence is an innate reflex in children and in many animal species like great apes, elephants, dolphins, and that examples of mutual aid between species do exist. Jean-Marie Pelt confirms this view in his book *La solidarité chez les plantes, les animaux, les humains (Solidarity in Plants, animals and humans)*, where he expands this demonstration on the entire living.

It is important to acknowledge that reactions necessary for convivence, like instinctive mutual assistance and recognition of interdependent ties, are at times instinctive or at least encouraged by nature itself. To put it otherwise, what these works reveal is that altruistic behavior are not dream-like delusions which would hope for a world like Noah's ark, a world where everyone is beautiful and kind; this behavior is possible, in the sense that it is inscribed deep down in our nature, in the genetic heritage of several species where each individual needs his peers to survive. Due to this, a feeling of empathy, according to Sandrine Musel, consultant in neuro-communication, is rooted in our genes: "It is about a natural and an instinctive aptitude, which is pre-programmed in social species".

A big collective movement for convivence is therefore possible. In fact, this movement is desirable, including a viewpoint which is strictly rational. At least this is what is pointed out by the economist, John Nash who received the Nobel Prize in 1994 for the development of a prominent balance that bears his name. Indeed, Nash made the most of the mathematical field of the game theory, to reveal that, in a game where each actor ignores the strategy of the other participants and where each player can choose among several options, the optimal balance is found when the player participants accept to choose a collaborative strategy. To put it otherwise, Nash's demonstration challenges the economic theory of the invisible hand, where each actor needs to try and maximize his very own interest: it's often more beneficial to bet on collaboration between various parties, for competition strongly threatens the possibility to maximize each one's profit. In the absence of implementing purely altruistic and selfless solutions, it can be said that the search for collaboration and fair agreement between all the parties seems to be more useful and profitable than egoism. To put it otherwise, convivence cannot be based solely on the altruism of others, but also on the pursuit of their well-understood interest.

Pillar of the family

Family is the first circle of convivence in which a human being evolves during the course of his life. It seems logical that relations between brothers and sisters, between parents and children condition the way of being or acting in all other social circles, whether this concerns work, friendly relations, relations with coreligionists or even relations that each citizen establishes with the jurisdiction or with a State, generally speaking.

Several studies have established a correlation between the way an individual behaves in the society with the family background. Emmanuel Todd, in his analysis called *Invention of Europe*, outlines a link in which various European people react when confronted with major historical events (Reform, Counter-Reform, French Revolution, Nazism…) and their family background.

The importance of family as being the matrix element is underlined by the sociologist Robert Fossaert who wrote: "Family dependence in which each man is born, does initiate language and teaches to adjust behaviors; but it is not an exceptional situation which would serve as a prelude to the free adventure of human individuals. It's only the first and most significant form of convivence from one's birth to death and no man can get away from this". Therefore, convivence is part of our destiny, right from the cradle until the end. The way a little boy receives love from his family circle, determines his capacity to receive and give, once the latter leaves the den.

This is what Ms. Annie Auret states, lawyer and president of la Maison de la parentalité (Parenting Home):

"Family is the fundamental unit of a society, a place where values are passed on, a place where the child identifies with himself, a place where young and old alike take refuge. [...] It is the first place where a new born receives love, it's a fundamental benchmark, it is a place where solidarity is expressed, where one learns to respect the other, [...] where creativity awakens but also a thirst for life; it is a refuge and the center link of social cohesion".

Pierre Bourdieu in *Esquisse d'une théorie de la pratique (Outline of a theory of practice)* seems to argue the extent of this family matrix, mainly by resuming an observation made by Antonio Gramsci: "a child's conscience isn't something unique [...]; it is the reflection of the spectrum of the civil society to which the child belongs, a reflection of social relations that is established in the family, entourage, in a village, etc.".

Whatever the extent might be, close or a broad one, that one gives to this relational matrix, one should take notice of its fundamental nature. However, the traditional relations of exchanging, sharing and passing onto the family circle have been deteriorated by several factors, which have appeared recently. Therefore, significant work is required to restore family ties. First and foremost, it is the parents' responsibility, but it is certain that the latters will need help from other social structures in order to spread the educational beacon, as many of them have forgotten how to love.

The first circle on which the family should lean on to rediscover unity, to become functional again is the one which immediately follows the family circle in the life of a child, to put it otherwise, school. An increasing proportion of parents apprehend school in a consumer-oriented manner today, in the same way as they expect to receive a product or a quality service when they buy something. They expect school to give them back a child, who is well educated when he or she leaves class. They refuse to accept their own responsibilities as time goes by and blame the educational failure of their children on the school system. Of course, the French education has a long way to go, when it comes to adapting to modern realities and giving itself the means to support children who are completely disoriented, but each one has to pitch in.

Alain Bouthier, from the parental committee of reflection of PEM meditation, has made a pertinent point in this matter: "We all need to understand the various means of belonging and participation to which the children are confronted on a daily basis at school. The French tradition of separation on the class-based threshold, which has put down roots in collective habits of teaching and parents, is a proof that convivence offers several evolutions, and the first one to benefit from these are children. Several leaders of school establishments foresee possibilities of involving the parents, but it is a completely different culture to combine mutual efforts of convivence among parents, family and the educational staff". It's a team effort between the teachers and family that shall make all the difference.

However, we should not neglect the role of grandparents in this re-conquering of a family unit and passing on love, not to mention knowledge, which comes along with it. Let us recall that contribution from the elders in educating the youngest ones has been vital for the development of the species, since prehistoric times. A symbiosis, an inter-generational convivence is not only possible but essential for our salvation. For this, one will need to repair the generational gap, revive a collaboration of the elderly with the youngest, to the fashion of our times. One will have to give back to the elderly the position that is owed to them in the society and to stop confining them in hospices through the pretext that one finds them unproductive and useless or that they aren't in keeping with the criteria of superficial beauty that one promotes nowadays. Their productivity can't be assessed in accounting terms; it's a verifiable fact when it comes to passing on their experience, knowledge and contributing their duty of remembrance against ignorance which seems to keep our fears alive.

Education and sharing knowledge

We saw that it is the reptilian mind, the primary emotion, which is nourished by conspiring theories, extremisms and all the simplistic and divisive messages that are spread around these days. This is also valid when it comes to historical revisionism, which even seems to question the reality of past mistakes and makes room for them repeating themselves. The mists of time keep emphasizing their symbolism, their aesthetics and thus tone down their terror. When it comes to a binary system that is so basic and is viewed as denial, with regard to History, one has to oppose the culture, its complexity but also its nuances.

In order to avoid conflation and for an abridged version to put down roots in the consciousness, a duty of remembrance needs to be realized. André Azoulay speaks about "anamnesis" work, which is firstly about writing down verbal traditions, to sustain the memory of first-hand witness of experiences in terms of convivence, those that are still vectors of a culture of exchange. Once the witnesses disappear, the verbal tradition won't be enough; therefore one needs researchers, scientists, and academics, to write this part of History on a solid medium. André Azoulay also insists on the necessity to create a link between cultures, mostly concerning mutual knowledge of Arab and Hebraic cultures. With this in mind, he founded the Aladin project, sponsored by Unesco that wishes to promote inter-religious dialogue. André Azoulay seems to mostly speak out against some visionaries who have taken Islam hostage: "The time has come for us to re-conquer these words in their diversity, when it comes to what is essential, that is to say, shared dignity, equality, freedom and the capacity of religions to communicate".

The best response to our nihilist obscurantism and simplistic democracy is education, development of the critical mind through training. Sharing knowledge shall dispel ignorance that breaks the world apart but also our capacity of living together. This sharing will bring along intellectual agitation, a growth of synergies for the benefit of everyone. An intellectual breeding ground in terms of research, mainly at the academic level would offer a two-fold advantage. Firstly, a practical advantage, as it would help forging ahead towards beneficial discoveries of the entire Humanity. Following this, a psychological advantage as it would trigger a habit to collaborate which, beyond the satisfaction of obtaining measurable and discernable results, will increase the desire to share and the notion of being part of everything. In this sense, passing on knowledge, cultural intelligence, discipline from one generation to the other, is a future building block.

A Personal Initiative

Creation of a Chair of Convivence

In order to remember the momentum that I advocate, I decided to create a Chair of Convivence, in 2016, placed under the patronage of Unesco. What is this exactly about? It can be defined as a spatiotemporal chair; this extra-curricular institution is made to forge partnerships between various actors of the society, and basically build a territorial, international and inter-generational network, to favor emerging innovations which are in keeping with societal changes. For example, the chair of convivence connects teachers, professional researchers, students (even from the first year of bachelors), associations, public or private companies to collaborate and materialize major projects.

What is the goal of this chair? What is its role? It is very ambitious as the aim is to change the educational paradigm and make it more collaborative, in continuity with the working lives and social, environmental and societal needs, etc. In a certain way, it's about moving from the conception of an educational system, which leans on knowledge, towards a conception that is more about transmission.

How can one do this? How can one organize this chair? To allow the true sharing of capacities of each and every person, for the benefit of everyone, we have come up with a network organization, on the "campus-*cluster*" model, forming "convivence clubs". What does this mean? Nothing but implementing a *cluster* of activities, connected with research and education but also public and private actors. Basically, it is about building depart-ments (nothing to do with competitivity but convivence), which are not just satisfied-unlike the start-up incubators today-, with gathering professionals but which also include students and researchers and motivated and dedicated citizens, to boost their exchanges in the field, for the benefit of a social or an environmental goal (which can or not, turn out to be profit-able for the concerned actors). Therefore, these clusters also include governmental institu-tions, local authorities, non-profit associations etc., and have the characteristic of bringing together dedicated individuals, regardless of their age, their profession or collegiate status, or even their interest (financial or altruistic).

These clusters aren't industrial clusters but *industrious clusters*: they don't necessarily have the vocation of creating products and then commercializing them, but they seek to create a convergence of skills, strengths and energies, available to carry out a project. This collation of researchers, enterprises of all sizes (local or exterior of a given territory), citizens favoring construction in symbiosis with a culture, is combined with innovation. Through personal construction but also conviction, I consider that students need to play a leading role in convivence clubs: their potential and their energy can help move mountains… Therefore, they are in the limelight within the system that extends according to four main axes:

— Involving extremely motivated students in research activities, as soon as they join campus, and not waiting until they are doing their Ph.D. Indeed, one realizes that the dedication of the best students in research activities usually takes place rather late during the curriculum. Their training shall significantly improve, and the research activities could benefit from this as well. Moreover, this corresponds to a current trend worldwide, whose aim is to better train and best utilize skills of *undergraduate* students (those who haven't obtained their bachelor's degree yet). Ecole des Mines in Alès in fact was the pioneer in this sector: 1990 onwards, the latter decided to directly assign its newcomers in their laboratories, producing a profound transformation of its educational model. This led to a broth of ideas of exceptional intensity and a fast-motion development of research results, through the creation of new companies. The California Institute of Technology, more popular under the name of Caltech, has also implemented a similar program, its well-known SURF (*Summer Undergraduate Research Fellowship)*, which has turned out to be remarkably efficient, because this program has generated several annual creations of promising start-ups. One needs to aim further than just simple laboratory internships, by considering that students who are well-prepared can very quickly turn into proactive forces, even if they haven't achieved their masters or Ph.D. yet.

– Student associations, student entrepreneurs and Ph.D. students for detecting actions and processing good projects. This action shall be the natural extension of the latter. The aim is to appoint the most active students at the heart of the innovation process. To do so, represent-atives specializing on precise themes will supervise student *task forces:* entrepreneurs and young students will provide support to expert researchers and increase the chance of an unconventional look on emerging projects. This measure will also help to immediately get together fifty or even hundreds of "homing devices", capable of giving their feedback in terms of observa-tion and reflection, if need be, as long as these students will themselves be dedicated in laboratories, as previously described. The action of these students and Ph.D. students during the maturation stage could also turn out to be decisive through their capacity of supporting prototyping operations, proof of concept, exploring the usage and markets, which shall also be very instructive.

– Developing student projects through various methods, in cooperation with their training establishments and the worlds of knowledge but also partner-ship. The concept of "developing student projects" (VPE in French) was certified IDEFI (Excellence in Education Initiatives) in March, at the initiative of Laurent Hua, while he managed ECE Paris, an Engineering grad school. This immediately concerned a thousand students and led to results which surpassed all expectations. VPE is about acknowledging the utility of student projects, beyond the academic framework. These projects can't be considered as simple educational exercises, but help find methods to concretely realize, under various forms, among which:

a. innovation in partnership with a company;

b. copyright, SOS Invention;

c. filing a patent application;

d. publishing (technical journals or speeches in national and international conferences);

e. creating start-ups.

If this last method is classic when it comes to awareness programs in terms of school entrepreneurship and implementing incubators, the first three are rather less, in regard to the educational level. Even so, according to Laurent Hua, VPE seems to be working well and has triggered great success. Innovation in partnership with a company, especially when it's properly organized, creates a new balance between youngsters and professionals, which increases energies and results. Without going into details, this kind of action can quickly establish very advantageous links between students and companies of all sizes, mainly SME/IMP. One still needs university institutions to accept and rearrange the schedule of students, for that reason. The Waterloo (Ontario) *cluster* could be considerd as a model: its "CO-OP" program, implemented by the university itself, was established at the heart of the industrial cluster of a few thousands of new technology SMEs'.

– The student association for international action of the campus. The students involved in this huge movement need to realize that it's a global movement. The current technologies favor quick and efficient formation of transnational teams, where students from various campuses come together. To show this, on my initiative and with the help of wonderful founding partners (Sabine Desnault, Philippe Laurier, Jean-Marc Pautras), committed to the same cause, several French universities but also some abroad, like Fes in Morocco, are considering to launch an extensive convivence operation, around a major theme, something I have been hobby-horsing for several years: autonomy. With this in mind, these universities have planned to welcome young people from all around the world on their campus, to conduct the initial exchanges.

This way, they'll have a work-force and unprecedented reflection at their disposal: thousands of students, among the better selected, nationally and internationally, who are enlivened by a common desire to collaborate and achieve a goal, which is of global importance.

The future of this chair is promising: prestigious sponsors join us to implement projects, carry out partnerships with these French and International universities, higher education establishments, secondary schools and high schools.

Everybody understands that in terms of innovation for example, the chairs of convivence and the associated *clusters* help expand and train the future breeding grounds of research and entrepreneurship.

A specific note for our chair of convivence, Europa Grande Region under the guidance of Professors Valerie Deshoulieres and Thomas Vercruysse, who work for the sustainable development and "convivence" on this cross-border territory, made up of Sarre, Lorraine, Luxemburg, Rhineland-Palatinate and Wallonia.

Attached to the University of Sarre, this chair aims to favor the cross-border academic cooperation (6 universities), in synergy with the institutional officers, locally elected representatives, municipal staff members, community networks, schools, the professional and industrial field. Its aim is to develop a campus-*cluster* of innovation, on a regional scale around unifying themes like ecology and autonomy.

Youth, ranging from collegiate to Ph.D. students, will therefore be associated to specific projects like environmentally sustainable management, both urban and rural, still rooted in the territorial reality. Persuaded that European construction can only be revived at the community level, we want people and generations to communicate in "convivence" clubs, to be able to highlight "places of remembrance" and to put the academic and technical capacities of each one, at the disposal of sustainable cross-border cooperation.

We are hoping to connect a future of knowledge with an ecosystem, which is concerned about its cultural and industrial heritage, in order to promote a sense of belonging, mainly regional which goes way beyond a European one. Our motto is "Each for all".

Therefore, I call upon all the higher education authorities to think about the development of such educational systems: combine strength and innovative energy of the youth with the competent management of professors and teachers, with the facilities provided by companies who wish to launch new products or services, which undoubtedly allow to establish a new economic and social balance, locally implemented but which is equipped with international resources, provided by convivence clubs. In fact, the companies are more and more aware of the importance of focusing on convivence through groups, as demonstrated by the initiative of André Renaudin, the general director of AG2R La Mondiale, who has just appointed a "convivence" officer in his company!

***

On the completion of this plea in which I had the audacity to claim certain positions, I would like to quickly go back to convivence and its necessity. Any approach of convivence is part of a sustainable strategy and can be implemented in all the sectors and segments of the civil society. Each one, with their own measures and means needs to reflect and contribute as well. I want to emphasize on the word *convivence,* as I think this word is a guide: the latter implies a new movement at the heart of ideas and ideologies. It shakes up existing ideologies and provides other means to express concepts, other means to understand concepts, other means to invent concepts. Therefore, a word is never neutral: it's a formidable weapon and I hope the one of convivence shall be: a weapon of *massive construction.*

***

"CONVIVENCIA" AND ITS EQUIVALENTS IN FRENCH AND ENGLISH. THE WORD AND NOTION

by Dominique-D Junod (Arbell),
Dr. in Political Science,
Lic. University of Geneva

The word convivencia is often and mostly used by historians, in Spanish, French and English, to designate the relatively harmonious coexistence, depending on the periods and the circumstances, which reigned between the populations of religions namely Christian, Jewish and Muslim, during the time of the Muslim conquest of the Iberian Peninsula and Septimania, towards the North, until "Reconquista" (711 1492.)

The concerned region and civilization that reigned were called "Al Andalus" and their capital was Cordoba. The cohabitation of religious communities living in Al Andalus was established by the Emirate and then by the Caliphate of Cordoba (Umayyad), based on the Koran. Non-Muslims, mainly Jews and Christians, were invited and even forced to accept legal pacts which conferred a status of "protected subjects" in the religious, cultural and economic fields. Coexistence among all these inhabitants, their convivencia, wasn't always easy and went through controversies between historians, but it is undeniably the intercultural and economic exchanges in various sectors which were remarkably productive and therefore allowed great personalities of the three religions to flourish and glow until today through their works, in the religious, artistic, medical, economic sector. Convivencia, whose first model was established in Cordoba, used to be and is still a significant and radiant contribution for the humanity, despite the dissensions between communities, rivalries, conflicts which couldn't always be avoided.

Nowadays, we refer more and more to this Golden Age of convivencia, even if it is a mythical representation of a blessed era at times, where an action or activity was carried out through dialogue, to promote a harmonious coexistence, whether it was among individuals or groups who wished to live together and maintain good relations, with respect to differences. This study deals with the word convivencia in Spanish (and Catalan), convivance in French (convivencia in Occitan) and convivence in English, but also the notion, which is part of the word. The approach shall be different depending on the language as each one has its own features and developments, that seem to condition the research and give rise to specific questions. This modest work which has been realized online, offers guidance for reflection and research…

Let's opt for an exercise and compare between convivencia, convivence, convivence and similar words: Why do we need the word convivencia (convivance, convivence?) The notion that these words express, is almost like that of "conviviality", "state of society "but can't be reduced to the latter: Hachette French Language dictionary dated 1987, gave the following definition of conviviality: "a liking for meals which unites many guests → "By extension: set of relationships of tolerance and exchange between people or groups who belong to the same society. And to add: in English, conviviality. "Coexistence" means sharing the same space through various people or groups of human beings. When a word is derived from Latin, it may have a static connotation and therefore doesn't force exchanges or doesn't necessarily look for them.

It is also reminiscent of the Cold War period and the concept of "peaceful coexistence". Way too respective, this word isn't really adapted to the spirit of Cordoba, which is expressed by the search for exchange and the blossoming of contacts. On the other hand, convivencia, * convivance, * convivence implies coexistence: indeed, for it to be invoked or sought after, at least two entities need to be on the same ground or territory. Anne Françoise Weber, author of a book on mixed couples (marriages between Muslims and Christians) in Lebanon, opts for conviviality (page 14 of the book), "in order to overcome the shortcomings of the term 'coexistence', which says nothing about the 'quality of relations' and friendliness, that refers to a' state of * society 'rather than' the action * of 'living * together'".

Convivencia, convivance, "convivence", implies conviviality and coexistence but goes way beyond this. The word "cohabitation" refers to cohabitation in the same space or to parties within a government. The word convivencia is used to designate cohabitation, Of course! for example, "Registro Civil" of Buenos Aires and of Murcia, issue a "Certificado * de * convivencia to those who are able to prove that they live in the same space".

That being the case, cohabitation is only one element of convivencia. What about the word "tolerance"? Tolerance means making an effort to accept those things one doesn't seem to accept, sometimes going beyond a form of contempt, a rejection. On the other hand, it is obvious that the action of tolerating is part of the convivencia approach.

One could continue the exercise with other terms to replace the word convivencia .... they are all more restricted than this one and their concepts are included in convivencia, which goes beyond the latter. Except perhaps the expression "living in togetherness": this English wording doesn't contain a tacit reference to convivencia in Cordoba and Al Andalus.

To conclude, the word convivencia was not used in Cordoba at the time of Caliphate of Umayas or even for that matter during the time of Al Andalus, however the concept of convivencia has been legally applied by Muslims, since the invasion of the Iberian Peninsula in the 8th century of our era. The word convivencia is a neologism and it is diffi-cult to find out since when it is being used, whether it is in Spanish, Occitan, French or English. Since the time of Al Andalus and Cordoba, the notion of convivencia has continued but also evolved.

Today, it represents a process of seeking harmony between people and populations living on the same territory. The word convivencia in Spanish is widely used, so is the word convivance in France. In Great Britain, the words convivencia and convivence are gaining ground. If we were to compare it to other words, such as coexistence, cohabitation, tolerance, usability etc., the term convivencia, convivance in French, convivence in English are obvious and therefore have no synonyms.

October 2012

***

Bibliographic Sources

Abélès Marc, *Politique de la survie,* Flammarion, 2006.

Bihouix Philippe and Mauvilly Karine, *Le désastre de l'école numérique. Plaidoyer pour une école sans écrans,* Seuil, 2016.

Blanchard Pascal, *La Fracture coloniale. La Société française au prisme de l'héritage colonial,* La Découverte, 2005.

Bouamama Said, "'Vivre ensemble' ou "vivre ensemble égalitaire"?", *Mediapart,* 3 Jan. 2017.

Bourdieu Pierre, *Esquisse d'une théorie de la pratique,* Librairie Droz, 1972.

Braudel Fernand, *L'identité de la France,* Paris, Le Grand Livre du mois, 2000.

Cederstrom Carl et Spicer André, *Le syndrôme du bien-être,* L'Échappée, 2016.

Clanet Claude, *L'interculturel – Introduction aux approches interculturelles en éducation et en sciences humaines,* University Press Mirail, 1988.

Couturier Brice, "Sois hypermoderne et tais-toi !", *Revue des Deux Mondes,* nov. 2016.

Faye Jean-Pierre, *Les langages totalitaires,* Hermann, 2014.

Fossaert Robert, *La société,* tome 6: "Les structures ideologiques", Cegep de Chicoutimi, coll. "Les classiques des sciences sociales", 1983.

Giraud Gaël (Economist): "La gouvernance des communs empêchera de privatiser l'humain", *Télérama*, 28 nov. 2016.

Gramsci Antonio, *Cahiers de prison*, Gallimard, 1978-1986.

Habermas Jurgen, *De l'éthique de la discussion*, translated from German by Mark Hunyadi, Flammarion, coll. "Champs", 1992.

Jaume Lucien, "La laïcité selon Jules Ferry", *Comment*, no. 155, autumn 2016.

Kepel Gilles, *La revanche de Dieu*, Seuil, 1991.

Laithier Stephanie, Conte Charles et Albert Jean-Paul, "Histoire des relations entre juifs et musulmans, des origines à nos jours" (educational support dossier), Ligue de l'enseignement, June 2014.

Lessig Lawrence, "Réseaux sociaux et démocratie: "Facebook et Twitter ne peuvent échapper à leurs responsabilités"", entretien au *Monde,* 9 dec. 2016.

Leloup Damien, "Un 'ami Facebook' n'est pas automatiquement un 'ami', selon la Cour de cassation", *lemonde.fr*, 16 Jan. 2017.

Maggiori Robert, *De la Convivance*, Fayard, 1985.

Maille Michel, "Citoyenneté et Convivance", Speech on 30 August 2005 at the opening of the university in summer: "Béziers ville citoyenne et médiatrice? Comment mieux vivre ensemble: la convivance", au FJT Claparède a Béziers.

Martin Laurent, "En France, on n'a plus le droit de rien dire !", *Revue des Deux Mondes*, nov. 2016.

MEDEB Abdelwahab, "Pour une religion de la 'paix perpétuelle'", *Le Monde*, 12 September 2008.

NASH John, *Essays on Game Theory*, Edward Elgar Publishing Ltd, 1997.

ONFRAY Michel, "Le venin du serpent devenu bipède", *Revue des Deux Mondes*, nov. 2016.

PELT Jean-Marie, *La solidarité chez les plantes, les animaux, les humains*, Fayard, 2006.

POOL James, *Who Financed Hitler*, Gallery Books, 1997.

RAWLS John, *Théorie de la Justice*, Seuil, trad. Catherine Audard, 1987 (1971, Harvard University Press).

AMARTYA Sen, *Ethics and Economics*, trad. Sophie Marnat, PUF, coll. "Quadrige", 2012.

RICARD Matthieu, *Plaidoyer pour l'altruisme*, Nil Éditions, 2013.

TODD Emmanuel, *L'invention de l'Europe*, Seuil, 1990.

Internet site on convivence:

<http://www.convivance-liens.com/Mona/articles.php?lng=fr&pg=2>, 26 February 2008.

www.ingramcontent.com/pod-product-compliance
Lightning Source LLC
Chambersburg PA
CBHW062227150726
47991CB00006B/2469